Help Bessie get home.

Draw a line that shows how she must go.

1

Help Lady Bird bring lunch to her chicks.

Draw a line that shows how she must go.

Help the fire truck get to the fire fast.

Draw a line that shows how it must go.

3

Help the diver find the treasure.

Draw a line that shows how she must go.

Help the calf find his mother.

Draw a line that shows how he must go.

5

Help Mama Bunny get home.

Draw a line that shows how she must go.

Mama Duck is looking for her ducklings.

Draw a line that shows how she must go.

Help the children find the eggs.

Draw a line that shows how they must go.

Help Charlie get down the hill fast.

Draw a line that shows how he must go.

9

Help the mailman deliver the mail.

Draw a line that shows how he must go.

Help the bear find her honey pots.

Draw a line that shows how she must go.

Help the baby animals find their mothers.

Draw a line that shows how they must go.

Help Betty get to the flower.

Draw a line that shows how she must go.

13

Help the miner get to the gold.

Draw a line that shows how he must go.

Help Sailor Sam get to the dock.

Draw a line that shows how he must go.

Help Ralphie find his bone.

Draw a line that shows how he must go.

Help the Clark family get to the tent.

Draw a line that shows how they must go.

Help Space Bunny get to his planet.

Draw a line that shows how he must go.

Help the ant get to the basket.

Draw a line that shows how she must go.

Help the dinosaur back to the trees.

Draw a line that shows how she must go.

Help Tina find her lion.

Draw a line that shows how she must go.

21

Help Tommy find his flashlight.

Draw a line that shows how he must go.

Help the mouse get home.

Draw a line that shows how he must go.

23

Help the zookeeper feed the monkey.

Draw a line that shows how he must go.

Help Mary find her lost puppy.

Draw a line that shows how she must go.

Help the clownfish find her school.

Draw a line that shows how she must go.

Help Betsy and Bruce get to Jane's party.

Draw a line that shows how they must go.

Help Papa Bear get home.

Draw a line that shows how he must go.

Help Mr. Fister get home to his pets.

Draw a line that shows how he must go.

Help Bucky the Clown get to his friends fast. ▬▬

Draw a line that shows how he must go.

Help Joey find his classroom.

Draw a line that shows how he must go.

Help the elephant get to her family.

Draw a line that shows how she must go.

Certificate of Achievement

Presented to

_____

_____

NAME

Great job on this **Get Ready!** workbook
from School Zone Publishing.

COOL!

Super!

Awesome!

Terrific!

Mazes

Children love mazes—and School Zone's are some of the most entertaining around. But mazes are more than fun—they develop eye-hand coordination, fine motor skills, attention to details, and thinking skills.

For more practice, choose these related School Zone products:

 Counting 1–10   Hidden Pictures   Does It Belong?

Review, Reinforce & Accelerate Learning!

All School Zone products are developed by skilled educators to provide the highest quality, up-to-date curriculum possible.

Workbooks
Top-quality content, clear directions, and full-color illustrations make School Zone workbooks the best choice. These workbooks cover essential curriculum from preschool through sixth grade.

Card Sets
Practice makes perfect! Engaging School Zone flash cards, game cards, and puzzle cards make learning lots of fun.

Start to Read!
Start to Read! books have predictable stories, rhyming words, limited vocabularies, and picture clues. Look for Start to Read! books on CD-ROMs, in sets, and as board books.

Mats
Colorful write-on, wipe-off mats can be used again and again. Topics include math, geography, the alphabet, and more.

Workbooks with CD-ROMs
Educational software delivers School Zone's quality content through the most current technology. Partnered with workbooks, these products build skills both on and off the computer.

Boxed Software
Subject-specific content makes School Zone software an ideal choice for young learners. Packed with puzzles, movies, and animated rewards, School Zone software is truly irresistible.

Flash Action Software
Flash Action transforms flash cards into exciting, interactive learning games that can be played independently or with a partner.

On-Track Software
School Zone workbooks are now in an exciting interactive format. The easy-to-use software provides audio guidance, tracks each child's progress, and features fun arcade games.

What's the Latest?

Check out our Web site at www.schoolzone.com to learn more about School Zone.